MW01706383

The Art of Appreciation

How to Appreciate Everything You Have and Take Nothing for Granted

Sanjana Ambegaonkar
Award Winning Author

The Art of Appreciation

www.theartofappreciationbook.com

Publisher
10-10-10 Publishing
Markham, ON
Canada

Printed in the United States of America

ISBN 978-1-77277-098-8

Contents

Dedication

I would like to dedicate this book to my grandparents.

"There is more hunger for love and appreciation in this world than for bread."

- Mother Teresa, Winner of the Nobel Peace Prize

Acknowledgements

First, I would like to acknowledge my Dad, Amit Ambegaonkar. My Dad helped me through every step of the way to make this book possible. I couldn't have done it without his help or encouragement. He is so positive and his wisdom can blow my mind at times. I am so blessed to be his daughter. Thank you Dad.

Next, I want to take a moment to thank my Mom, Swapna Ambegaonkar. I wouldn't be the person I am today without her unlimited amount of love, guidance and patience for me. I respect her so much, and I am so grateful to have her. Thank you Mom.

Thank you to my little brother, Sahil, for being positive and making me feel like a role model. Thank you to my aunt, Shilpa Dalvi, and uncle, Hemant Dalvi, who believe in me and always support me in all my undertakings. Thank you to my cousins, Pranali Dalvi and Prachiti Dalvi, my role models, who are always there to guide and support me. Thank you family.

I would like to thank my friends. Their encouragement had such a big effect on this book, because they kept cheering me on and supporting me. Their "wows" are what kept me on track. Thank you friends.

I would like to thank all of my teachers, right from junior kindergarten to now. It is because of them that I have developed the passion for learning and expressing my thoughts through literature. Thank you teachers.

Now, I would love to thank Mr. Raymond Aaron. He is one of the best mentors, and he has impacted my life like no other. I was able to write this book because he taught me the ideas and concepts through his training. I love the fact that Raymond teaches very important concepts in such a way that it is easy to understand. Thank you Raymond.
I would like to acknowledge Rosa Greco, my book architect. I genuinely could not have finished this book without her advice, guidance and encouragement. Her emails were inspiring and she knew exactly what to do no matter what. Thank you Rosa.

Above all, I want to truly appreciate you as the reader of my book. The reason for expressing my special appreciation to you is that, even though this topic is not a new topic, you still took the time and effort to buy and read this book. There are a lot of different ideas discussed in this book, and I hope you learn a lot!

About the Author

Sanjana is very passionate about sharing her ideas, and believes in helping others improve their lives. At the very young age of 12, she is very well educated about some of the aspects of life that even adults find very fascinating.

This book is a result of such an idea that Sanjana wanted to share with all her readers to help them understand this critical and important facet of their lives.

The valuable concept of appreciating how lucky we are has been in her mind for a long time. In grade 3, she was told to write a story about anything she wanted, and she chose the topic "Surviving without cell phones." The moral of the story was that we are so lucky to have these modern-day technologies.

In grade 5, she had to do a project about water as a useful resource. She added extra credit by connecting it with a life lesson, which was how lucky we are to have resources.

In grade 7, Sanjana was selected from her school to compete at the provincial level to do a speech, on - "Children in the 21st Century are Lucky." Her speech was about considering ourselves lucky to have a lot of resources and technologies at our fingertips.

So, when Sanjana decided to write a book, she almost immediately knew what her book was going to be about! It was the same concept that she has been talking, writing and sharing about for so many years - Appreciation.

Due to her understanding of the idea, and her achievement of success by using this outstanding quality, she is very pleased to put together such a spectacular book. Over the past few years, she has been receiving great teachings from different coaches and mentors that solidified her belief in appreciation.

Sanjana, therefore, puts forth the idea that, although appreciation is a commonly used trait, if used in the book's methods, it will enhance your life and the life of others around you.

Foreword

I am delighted to endorse Sanjana Ambegaonkar's book, *The Art of Appreciation.* In my teachings I give very high importance to gratitude and validation. These are the highest values that you can have towards others.

I am very happy and excited for Sanjana, for understanding the concept at the early age of 12 years old, and for actually implementing it in her life. *The Art of Appreciation* has been written to help you benefit from Sanjana's experiences and to enrich your mind with her knowledge and expertise.

I am confident that you will find this book truly inspirational, and the insights discussed here are sure to add value to your life.

I strongly recommend that you read and implement the strategies and ideas put forth in this book.

Raymond Aaron
New York Times Bestselling Author

Chapter 1

APPRECIATION - AN ART

Thank you! Merci! Gracias! 谢谢! Grazie!

Thank you is such a familiar term for all of us. We use it regularly in day-to-day conversations in our lives. It is used so commonly all over the world.

Thank you is one of the first words that children learn when taught to speak. Whenever something was done for us, our parents would encourage us to say thank you. Saying thank you is one of basic manners that we have to develop. As a child, do you remember the answer to the traditional question, "What do you say?" Ever since then, we have continued to use this word. Let's think about this for a second.

Over all these years, has the real purpose of thank you changed for you? Is saying, "Thank you" just a habit or is it expressing your gratitude? Thank you has been tossed around so many times but hardly anyone knows the true value and effect of this word.

The Question of Why

Why is it so important to use these words, when there are more than a million words in the English language? Why is it a necessity to say something to the person holding the door for you? Well, what if you didn't? Imagine if you said absolutely nothing to the person who gave you a gift for your birthday. The person would feel bad and would regret buying you the gift. That person may never know what the reason for not getting acknowledged was. It is therefore so important to recognize and enjoy what other people do for you.

According to the Merriam Webster dictionary, the definition of appreciation is, "A feeling of being grateful for something; an ability to understand the worth, quality, or importance of something; an ability to appreciate something." But what if appreciation meant much more than that? If you carefully study the definition, you may realize that appreciation is not such a common occurrence. As you can see in the definition, the word appreciation has much deeper meaning than just a regular "Thank you." There are so many things around us that we may take for granted. Right now, I want you to think about five simple things that you are grateful for. It could be anything. Just look around or think about and name five things.

Appreciation can be being grateful for the things that you have but also, what if we were appreciative to the source of the things that we are grateful for? The source for everything you just listed is people. Think of clean water. Clean water has to be filtered by filtrating systems. Hundreds of people put their time and effort into making them. If you are thankful for your house, think of everyone from the architects to the builders that spent a lot of their time and effort on your building. Trace everything on your list back to the human source and just thank whoever was the reason for you having this necessity.

Reasons to Appreciate

Appreciating is so important, because most people believe the media when they state that it is such a scary world we live in, but if you look around and smile at everyone and everything and realize how lucky you are to have all this, it won't be scary anymore. Just by smiling, you make other people's lives better. A smile is like a gift. If you smile at someone, you're giving him or her a gift. They give you a smile, or thank you, back. When people smile back, you get the same fulfilled feeling as you would when someone likes a gift that you gave them.

Another essential reason to appreciate is respect. When you appreciate, people will respect you for saying good things about them, which they may not have even realized. You are showing an interest in them by noticing the good things they've done, so they will like and respect you.

One of the laws of the universe is that whatever you give, you get back. This is also true when it comes to appreciating. When you give someone a compliment, they will pass on the gesture to someone else. It will be like a boomerang. You throw it; then it goes around and comes back.

One of the best parts about appreciating is that it is completely free. Appreciation is one of the unique attributes that has such a huge impact and does not cost even a penny! Do you know anything else that can do that? It doesn't cost anything to tell someone a good thing, or appreciate someone for what he or she did or who they are. People will do more for recognition than for money. That's how powerful appreciation is.

If there are so many benefits from appreciating, why do people not do it? Why can't people appreciate to gain respect? Why can't people throw the boomerang to get it back? Why can't people say a few words for free? Why can't people take one simple step towards a brighter world? People are scared.

It can be difficult to say anything without being judged. You have to be able to ignore what others think about what you say. Appreciating doesn't come easily to everyone. It takes courage to say something and not care if others criticize you. This is hard because you have to ignore the looks or remarks that anyone makes.

"Art is not what you see, but what you make others see."
Edgar Degas.

With appreciation, you make the person see what they needed and make them feel special. Appreciation is an art because it takes a lot of creative skill and imagination. You have to be creative and have an imagination of what you compliment people on. You can't let people judge your art or change what it looks like, just as you can't let people judge your words or change what you say.

Life is not promised tomorrow, and just thinking about that makes us realize how precious living is. In order to have a brighter future, you have to be able to ignore the criticizing that people do and make people happy by spreading appreciation.

Notes

Notes

Notes

Notes

Chapter 2

#BLESSED

"Be thankful for what you have;
you'll end up having more.
If you concentrate on what you don't have,
you will never, ever have enough."
Oprah Winfrey

I was restless. I felt uneasy and scared. It's lost! I can't live without it! How am I going to survive? I looked to my left. I looked to my right. Not there. Why did this place have to be so big? It could be anywhere. I looked on my bed. I ran downstairs. I looked in the sofa. I looked in my big kitchen. Not there. Now I was panicking. Where is it? My heart was beating faster than a racecar.

My mom looked at me strangely. "Are you okay?" she asked me. "Mom! Dad! I lost it! I've been looking for it for ten minutes, and I can't find it anywhere!" I replied worriedly. My dad gave me a confused expression. "What are you looking for? What are you so stressed about? What's missing?" "MY PHONE!"

Today, we are so blessed to have resources and technologies that other people can't have. In the past, people lived their whole lives without these things but today we can't live one day without them, like me without my phone for only ten minutes! We rely on things that we don't even realize, especially important resources like clean tap water, fresh air, and clothing. Even the fact that we live in a safe and peaceful environment shouldn't be taken for granted. We are so grateful to have such a great lifestyle in this generation.

Consider Yourself Lucky

The first reason to consider yourself lucky is the advancements in technology. Think about it. If you were driving from Toronto to New York, would you actually print out directions? Probably not, because of the global positioning system, or the GPS. Not only would it give you directions on where to go, but it would also give you information along the route. If you got hungry, it would guide you to a nearby restaurant. If you needed a gas refill, your GPS would lead you to a gas station. What if you missed a turn? No worries, the GPS has your back!

Medical equipment is another necessity that we rely on to survive. According to a 2011 World Health Organization study, there are more than 150 different types of medical equipment used just to find out the problem that doctors need to fix with your body. Because of all this equipment, everyone is living healthier, happier, and longer lives.

What about cell phones? Could we survive without cell phones? There have been countless incidents when phones saved lives. Cell phones are no longer considered a luxury. In fact, they are a requirement for our everyday lives. Phones have applications that have different uses. These apps are not necessities, but they are helpful. Apps help you throughout the day. For communication, entertainment, awareness, and much more.

In the future, there will be even more technologies, that we don't need to survive, but could be extremely useful. Drones that can deliver food, flying cars that can make traveling much easier, and virtual reality technologies that can make you go where you want to be. These are ideas that are starting to exist already, so who knows what the future can hold?

We have all these things, and yet some people spend too much time looking for more, instead of appreciating what they already have. Right now, I want you to step outside, look at the sky, and just contemplate how amazing life is. See the beauty around you. Think about people who make you happy. Think about sunshine. Think about the amazing moments in life, from holding a baby, to finding something you lost.

Looking at The Bright Side

It feels good to look at the bright side of everything. You realize how great your life is. Life is a bundle of little things, and when you appreciate them, you get more good things. The little things could be anything. A fresh coffee in the morning, a good talk with a friend, or just a little smile and compliment from (or to) a stranger. If you only get happy from the big things, like getting a new house, new car, or getting a promotion, you will rarely be happy. The big things happen much less often and that is how sad people stay sad. They wait for big things to happen instead of appreciating what they already have. Instead of waiting for things you want, appreciate the little things that happen to you.

Everyone wants to appreciate, but unfortunately, we often forget everything we have, and to be thankful for it. Instead of counting our blessings, like many people say we should, we tend to count the bad things, and complain about how unlucky we are. Life is a gift that doesn't last forever. And before life takes away from us what we take for granted, we need to change how we think. Instead of focusing on what we need in life, we need to recognize the mindset that what we already have is enough.

3 Keys of Appreciation

There are three steps on how to start appreciating and stop taking things for granted:

1. Live in the moment. "The past is full of tears and the future is full of fears" –Unknown. To stop taking things for granted, we need to stop thinking about regrets and missed opportunities of the past. When we think about the future, we think about what should and shouldn't happen, and we try to control what will happen. We have to live in the present, and then we can notice what we have and take nothing for granted.

2. Notice your surroundings. In this generation, sadly, all we see is what's on our screens of technology and media. We pay more attention to the screen than the real life around us. Because of this, we forget what's important. The people in our lives, work we have to do, experiences, and

the things we have. Make it a habit to look around and realize what you have. First notice the big things, like your job, home, and family. Then, the small things, like the food you eat, the water from your faucet, and the human senses you have.

3. Help others. Helping others will make other people happy, and you will get a thank you, or at least a smile back. That warm fuzzy feeling when you help someone is worth appreciating for. Not only does helping others mean charity, it could be helping friends, family members, or even a stranger. The fulfilling feeling will make you happy, and helping the person will make them happy. Just by helping others you can make the world a better place.

Gratitude and Abundance

"Gratitude creates abundance. Complaining creates poverty."
Unknown

The life you want is the life that you already have. Gratitude can transform your entire life. No matter how bad someone's life is, if they look hard enough and find something to be grateful for, their life will improve. You have to be grateful for what you have and not complain about anything. Complaining is focusing on the negative problem.

If you want to lose the awesome things in life, if you want to have more and more problems everyday, if you want to be unloved and lose your relationships, all you have to do is complain. However, if you want to have an amazing life, if you want a lot of money, and if you want to surround yourself with people you love, all you have to do is be grateful.

A Memorable Experience

I was recently at the coffee shop in a hospital. I was waiting in line thinking what to order. I looked around at what people were ordering and what looked appealing. I looked in front of me and I saw a little boy, about age 7 with blond hair and blue eyes, looking at me. I smiled. I glanced down and saw that he had a prostate leg. He saw me look at it and smiled.

I was embarrassed because he must've seen my jaw drop when I looked down at his leg. I thought he would say something about how it happened, or how it hurt. But he surprised me and said, "Cool, right?" I nodded my head. "I want a hook on it like Captain Hook has on his hands, but my mom said no," he said.

I was amazed. What an incredible attitude to have even when faced with such unfortunate circumstances.

"Gratitude is the best attitude."
Unknown

He was making the best possible outcome of his situation. This incident had a big impact on my life because whenever I am faced with a problem I just say the words, "Captain Hook" and it helps me find the best out of my situation.

Next time, when you are faced with an adversity, just think of this boy's imagination and creativity to come up with an idea of how to solve your problem, or at least make it easier.

A Huge Takeaway

After he left, I talked with my friends and we all thought wow, no ordinary person would say this; normally people would say something negative. What he said was special, and definitely not expected. This made me realize the value of this quote:

"Trade your expectation for appreciation and the world changes instantly."
Tony Robbins

Expectation is also looking forward to what you want, or looking back in the past at what you did or did not receive. There is no present time in expectation. Appreciation is just about right now and what is around. If you are throwing a party, don't expect the guests to show up at the time on the dot; instead appreciate that they made an effort to come and spend time with you.

When you move your energy from future to present, you will shift the energy around what you want and bring it into the present moment. You'll feel better, and make other people feel better too. This is not easy, as it takes patience to be okay with other people's choices. You have to find the good in the situation.

It's All a Choice

Is appreciation easy or hard? For some people it's easy to appreciate things. but for other people, the opposite is true. Your attitude is your choice. You can choose how you react to things and people. You have to be able to use your imagination and create a solution to your problems. This is why appreciation is an art. It takes creative skill and imagination to come up with a way to make a bad situation good.

It's your choice. You can either complain about how hard life is and how much pain is in your life, or you can use your imagination to come up with a different perspective.

Notes

Notes

Notes

Notes

Chapter 3

PERSPECTIVE MATTERS

"The things you take for granted, some people are praying for."
Marlan Rico Lee

Perspective. Say it out loud. What comes to mind? People's point of views, a different prospect, or someone's writing style. But what about art? Perspective is a major part of any art piece. Artists spend a lot of time perfecting the detail in the art piece, and when they step back and look at it with a different perspective, it looks much better and makes them feel that they have achieved something.

Two months ago, I had to make a sculpture out of many materials for school. When I was working on it, I didn't realize how good it would look because I was too focused on my perspective. I was stressed that it would look choppy and messy, but when I looked at it from the front and from afar, I realized that it wasn't as bad as I thought. It made me feel much better about myself, and I felt proud. To explain my point further, here are a few examples of art that looks amazing from one perspective, but normal from another. To someone looking at this from the side, it looks quite strange and unappealing. They have to be able to see things from another perspective to understand the beauty in it.

For this first one, on the side it just seems like cut up pieces of paper. But if you look at it from the front, it is a lady smiling with perfect shading and proportions.

In this second one, from the front, it probably looks a normal metal fence. However, when you look at it from the angle like in the below picture, you can see that it is a creatively painted portrait of a woman's face.

A Perspective: "How Are You Doing?"

My dad used to work in a hospital as a physiotherapist, and he took care of patients with injuries. Once, he had to treat a man about 28 years old.

His back was hunched, and he had a scowl on his face. My dad asked him how he was, and he replied, "Horrible. My back feels like it will collapse. And oh, the pain. It's like this nasty needle in my back. Why did this have to happen to me?"

My dad's next patient was in the Intensive Care Unit. The ICU is a special department in the health care facility. It is where critical patients get treated for their medical conditions. When he went to treat the patient in ICU, he saw an old lady with many tubes and monitors connected to her body. She was lying on her back on the hospital bed. My dad walked over to her and saw her smiling through her oxygen mask. My dad asked her how she was. Even through her oxygen mask, she replied, enthusiastically, "Great!"

Your problem may seem huge to you, but other people could have much bigger problems. The man's back pain was so small, but he chose to complain and act like there was no more life left to live for him. However, the old lady was in her worst condition of her life, and she said she felt great. If the younger man looked from the older lady's perspective, he would've realized that he should've been grateful that his pain was merely a back pain. This is how perspective matters.

The Solution to Every Problem

There is always someone, somewhere, wishing they had what you have. When you are faced with a problem, just think about how you are lucky that it is small, and that you are so fortunate because it could've been much worse. That is looking from a different perspective.

Just take a breath and realize that somewhere, someone could be taking their last breath. Stop complaining and look from a different perspective. Learn to live life with what you have and a positive attitude about it.

It is not always easy to do that when you're in very unfortunate situations. Even for me sometimes, it is hard to replace all my negative thoughts with positive ones. So let me share with you what has worked for me in really dreadful situations. I purposely compare myself to other children who face more struggles in their lives than me.

People in underprivileged countries face problems that we can't even imagine, and the absolute least we can do is appreciate what we are so lucky to have. Don't take the things and people that you have been blessed with for granted.

In the past, not just adults, but children have had to walk long distances just to get clean drinking water. However, these children considered themselves lucky if they compared themselves to those involved in child labor, working hard and causing mental or physical damage to their bodies.

I was shocked to find out from a UNICEF International report that there are still more than 250,000 child soldiers around the world today. The closest that kids in developed nations have been to experiencing wars is playing fighting video games, like Call of Duty.

This is one of the many reasons to appreciate everything that we have, from 6000 movies available on Netflix, to clean tap water in your water bottle.

The Problem Perspective

Digging deeper into this concept, what are our generation's problems? Wi-Fi is not working? Earphones tangled? Battery low? Cold water when showering? Breaking news. Those are not problems. First world problems aren't difficult situations. They are pointless things to complain about. They do not affect our lives in any major way.

How do we, in developed countries, get water? Well, we can walk to the kitchen sink, get a cup, and pour water in the cup. And most people take it for granted! Most people find it painful to just pay for the water, imagine how sore and tired they would get walking hours for it. In some countries, people have to walk for hours to get clean water, and when they find it, they have to carry the water on their heads. In Sudan, they use 400 liters for 20 people, while in Canada; we use the same amount for one person in one day.

One third of the world's population lives in places with water shortages. Think about how lucky we are to have access to water whenever we want. You use water more than you think. To brush your teeth, you use about 5 gallons of water. It takes a lot of water to produce food. For 1 kilogram of bread, it takes 1000 liters of water. To simply flush a toilet, it takes 1.5-4 gallons of water.

We use this much water, and some people take it for granted. They waste water without thinking about the consequences. Water is the most valuable resource on Earth, and we have to take care of it. Without water, there would be no life in this world. This is why we need to acknowledge how fortunate we are to have this resource.

In other countries, you have to pay for your own healthcare, and it is not advanced. Here, it is so advanced, and yet people still manage to complain about the little drawbacks. Just think of the knowledge of doctors, nurses, and healthcare professionals. Think about the technology. We are so lucky to be healthy. To have a heart that pumps blood to every part of your body and to help us feel. To have lungs for letting us breathe and live.

It's amazing to have these resources, if you think about it. As technology develops, we gain more and more knowledge about how many things we have, so we should also gain knowledge about how fortunate we are to have these things. Sometimes we forget to appreciate everything we have. This is when we have to be able to look at things from someone else's perspective. When we see others' perspectives, they could be worse than ours, so we can be happy with our perspective.

Now that we have discussed the basics of appreciation, let's dive into the details.

Notes

Notes

Notes

Notes

Chapter 4

THREE STAGES OF APPRECIATION

"Life's too short not to show
your love to someone or something."
Patrick Driessen

This book is special because it has a secret that no other book has. It holds the key to happiness. It is an essential part of a brighter future. This book contains a recipe for happiness, for you and everyone around you. Are you ready? Ready for the answer to one of the deepest questions in life, "How do you give people value?" Ready to learn the unique understanding of appreciation? Ready to react to bad situations better?

Well first, let's think about some things. I want you to fill in the chart on the next page with five things that people do for you, and how you react to them. For example, if they hold the door for you, write *hold door - I smile and say thank you*. On the left column, write what people do for you. On the right column, write how you react. Keep going until you have 5 things to think about. Be 100% honest.

	Things people do for you	How do you react to what they do
EX.	*Hold door*	*I smile and say thank you*
1		
2		
3		
4		
5		

This chart will help you throughout the next few chapters. Perhaps by the end of this book, you will change the way you react to the things people do.

Spectrum of Interaction

The concept of "The Spectrum Of Interaction" is one of the rare things that you will find in this book and nowhere else. This diagram shows the different ways that people react to an action being done for them. There are five different levels of how to react to people.

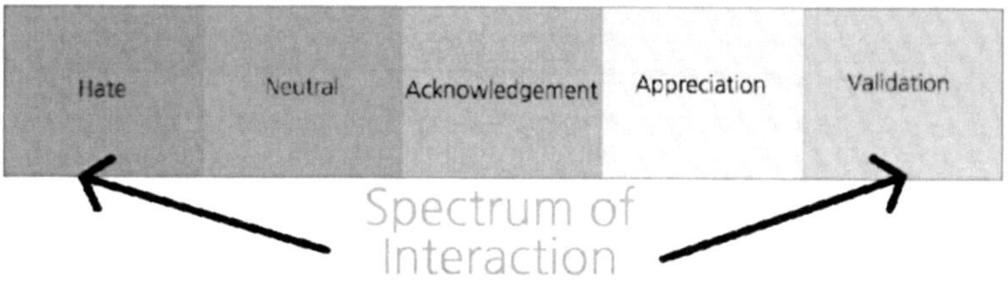

The first is hate. This is responding negatively to people. This is absolutely the worst thing you could do. In my example of holding the door, reacting with hate would be giving them a nasty look or saying something along the lines of, *"Why would you do that? I could've done that myself."* The other person would get offended and feel negatively about you. There is no real reason to respond with hate unless they hurt or disrespect you.

The second section is neutral. This would be saying nothing and not reacting to the person. For the door example, if you just walked through door without realizing their existence, it is neutral. The person would feel strange and feel that you didn't appreciate their kind gesture.

Neutral is like the number 0. It has no positive or negative value. It is doing nothing, but it is better than negative and worse than positive. It is not helping the person feel good, but not giving them a disagreement. Rather than feeling mad or sad, they would feel awkward. You want them to feel happy. People want value. By staying neutral, you make them feel invisible. This could ruin their entire day and they will have no respect for you.

Now let us look at the three very important stages of appreciation.

1. Acknowledgement
2. Appreciation
3. Validation

Usually, we do not consider appreciation happening in stages. The reason for this is that maybe we look at appreciation as a verb and treat it very superficially.

Taking A Closer Look

I would encourage you to have a closer look at the concept of appreciation, and realize that it's not just an utterance to throw around, but it has a much deeper and more important meaning. Once you understand these stages, you will realize what stage of appreciation you are in, and this will help you understand appreciation better.

Understanding these stages will also help you understand how you could use the concept of appreciation in your future interactions with people. This will help you in forming better relationships, connections and bonds with others.

What is the most important thing people need? That sounds like an extreme question that has such a complicated answer. No. It is so simple. People need love. Not money. Nothing fancy. Just love. We all need to love others and be loved. Everyone is human, and we can forget that we are not the only ones with problems. The only way you can receive love is if you have relationships. The three stages helped me improve all of my relationships, because I sent my love to everyone. No matter who they were. The people who we don't appreciate are the ones who need the most love. That is the only way you can have a great relationship with everyone. Eventually, the ones you love are the only ones that matter. It doesn't matter if you're poor, rich, famous, hated. All that matters is that there are key people who are there for you. This can be a hard concept to grasp. Everyone will have a moment when this clicks. A genius moment. A moment where time stops and you feel on top of the world. You are surrounded by loved ones, and realize that's all that matters.

All you need to do now is interact positively.

Notes

Notes

Notes

Notes

Notes

Chapter 5

RECOGNITION & ACKNOWLEDGEMENT

"Making one person smile can change the world. Maybe not the whole world, but their world. Start small. Start now."
Unknown

Recognition is the very first stage in appreciation. Recognition is better than neutral but a step lower than acknowledgement. Recognizing is realizing something exists. For example, if a friend gives you a present, recognizing it would be realization of the gesture of the friend. You would enjoy the gift and just know that the person gave you the gift rather than interacting with the friend.

Acknowledgement is a step above that. It is when you notice and accept that you have something or have had something done for you. For the example I used above, acknowledging is when you notice the person and gift and accept that they have done something for you, and you smile at them.

Even the lowest stage of appreciation causes a smile. It's so important to acknowledge the person because, no matter what it was, they had to have put some time or effort into it. Think of if they hadn't done whatever it was. How would it have changed your day? If your hands were full, someone might've held the door for you. If they hadn't opened it, you could've dropped something in the difficult process and hurt yourself. Be thankful that the person was there right when you needed them.

The Source

It's easier appreciating things than people. That's a set in stone fact. It can be hard to appreciate the thing rather than the person. This is why you have to be able to look at the source of everything. When you eat an apple, think of the person who planted the tree. Think about the farmers who watered and made sure the plant was cared for. Think about the grocery shop staff that provided such a variety of apples.

It's amazing how we are just able to skip the credits in a movie. Those people are the reason the movie exists. Think about not just the cast, but think about the technical departments, the filming teams, or the wardrobe managers. There are so many people who have made the movie what it is today. We just take the source's effort for granted and we criticize the movie and forget about all the time and effort that the movie has taken from so many people.

When reading this book, think of not only the author's many hours put into writing the book, but think about publishing company staff who found a cover, printed hundreds of copies, and made the book that you are holding right now. For any book, so much effort and time has been put into it. We fail to recognize that, and focus instead on whether we liked the book or not.

"Three billion people on the face of the earth
go to bed hungry every night,
but four billion people go to bed every night hungry
for a simple word of encouragement and recognition."
Robert Cavett

Are you one of those people? Would a simple recognition help you fall asleep peacefully? You are not the only one. Not many people receive acknowledgement, because people are only worried about their problems, and their own road to safety. They don't look around to see others struggling as well. If people worked together, acknowledged problems and offered solutions, there would be less worrying and stress.

I asked my mom if she had any juicy stories from her childhood that I could incorporate in my book. She had to think for a long time before she realized there were no big stories that stuck in her mind. Now, the story is different. My mom has learnt from her mentors to acknowledge.

Think about every night you could've slept so much more peacefully if you had a few words of recognitions or encouragement. Even a smile would have been nice. But that night will never happen again.

Once you start acknowledging others, you will get it back. You will be acknowledged for everything, even just a small thing like smiling at a stranger.

Even if we are talking about huge appreciation gestures, do not underestimate the power of a simple thank you. As you will see, a simple thank you also has a special place in the world of appreciation.

Notes

Notes

Notes

Notes

Chapter 6

THE VALUE OF THANK YOU

"Feeling gratitude and not expressing it is like wrapping a present and not giving it."
William Arthur Ward

Most people get up to this level and they think they know everything about it. But they don't. What people don't know is that, in this level, there is still a way in which you can step up your thank you game.

At this stage, the importance of thank you is key. When someone gives you a gift, you tend to say, "Thank you so much!" Period. That is great, but doesn't the person who dedicated time and effort towards you deserve a little bit more?

Well, this is a unique way to improve just those four words. There is a way to leave the person as happy as you are, and a way to express extra gratitude, because there is no limit to gratitude.

Small Word, Huge Impact

We are now going to consider a small word in the English dictionary that can totally change the value of gratitude you express. It is a three-letter word that we use on a regular basis - a word that can enhance all your appreciation interactions. All you have to do is say the word "for." That's it! Instead of saying just, "Thank you so much," what if you said, "Thank you for this gift, I really appreciate it!" Adding those extra words makes your gratitude seem much more valuable.

It is also so great, because it makes the statement specific. Imagine someone just gave an amazing, knowledgeable, and interesting presentation. You liked it so much. Acknowledging that would be keeping it to yourself without giving any feedback. Appreciation would be saying "Thank you." The next step in appreciation would be, "Thank you so much for giving this informative and interesting presentation! It helped me a lot!"

Think about if you were the person giving the presentation. Which response would you like to receive the most? The last one. Appreciation is so great because it is enjoying the good qualities of everything and being grateful for them.

Appreciation Statistics

Studies show that 46% of employees leave their place of employment because they feel unappreciated. 61% said their bosses don't show much importance to them, and 88% said they do not receive acknowledge for the work they do. We need to help those 88% of people to feel appreciated.

Effective Ways to Appreciate

And there are many ways we can do that. Expressing your appreciation can be difficult because you might think it's awkward, or useless. But it makes a huge difference in people's lives. Here are 10 examples of how you can express your appreciation to people:

1. **Flowers** - Imagine hearing a doorbell and opening the door to a bunch of bright, fresh flowers that smell heavenly. How great would that be? Now, imagine that it is you causing that much happiness to another person. Giving unexpected flowers is a unique and special way to show your appreciation.

2. **Thank you notes** - Thank you notes can make a huge difference in people's lives. Whether it's giving one to

a teacher who you appreciate, or if it's someone that you work with, it's a great way to show your appreciation.

3. **A Lagniappe** - A lagniappe is a small gift that shows your gratitude. Leaving one on someone's desk, or mailing one, can make the person feel special. Receiving a gift on Christmas or on your birthday is great, but getting a gift unexpectedly creates an even better feeling.

4. **Larger tip** - A great way to show your gratitude towards a business or somewhere that served you well is leaving a bigger tip than usual. It's the small things that make people happy, and the look on people's faces when they see that you have gave them a surprise tip is magical.

5. **Leave a note** - Whenever we travel, my family always stays in a hotel room. Ever since I was seven years old, I would make a little note of gratitude to leave in the room when we left. I would leave it in a space that was visible, so that when the cleaning staff came in, they would see the note and be happy that they were acknowledged for what they do. Now, not only has my writing got much better, but I also leave notes in other

places, like restaurants, stores, and anywhere else that I liked the products or services.

6. **Random act of kindness** - The little things are the things that people remember for the entire day, or maybe their entire life. A great example would be, recently, when my friend was in the drive-through line of Tim Hortons. When she got to the register, the lady working there told her that the person in front of her had paid for her order. This made her and her mother very happy, as they had gotten what they wanted for free. They felt very lucky and grateful for the kind stranger.

7. **Feedback on websites** - Some companies are very online friendly, and if you give a positive rating or review about a certain post, they will be grateful, and their bosses might notice and give them a promotion. They will be even more grateful because you were the reason for their achievements.

8. **Employee positivity** - If you really like the service from somewhere, and you feel that they need recognition and appreciation, you can write a note to the boss to tell him or her that the employee is doing an impeccable job.

9. **Let the boss know they are doing a good job** - Employees can get validation from their bosses or other staff members. But what about the bosses themselves? Who would they get appreciation from? Write them a short letter or an email telling them what you like about the service or products, and it will make their day a lot better.

10. **Surprise mail** - When I get mail, I get very curious. It is one of the exciting parts of my week. It may sound silly, but it is a common thing that people do. Opening your mail and finding a gift or a letter can be so satisfying. My aunt travels a lot, and whenever she does, she sends a postcard from wherever she is. It can be very entertaining seeing what she is doing, and it is so cool to learn about different systems and cultures.

Wow. Doesn't it feel like we've come a long way in understanding appreciation? Even if you are able to apply the techniques and principles discussed so far, you will be way ahead of others. However, if you read and apply what's coming next, you will see outstanding results in your life. If you're ready, let's move on.

Notes

Notes

Notes

Notes

Chapter 7

THE APPRECIATION PEAK - VALIDATION

You are amazing. You are thoughtful. You are creative. You are great. You are absolutely incredible. I'm so glad you have affected my life. Thank you for being such an amazing human being. Thank you for being so positive. Thank you for being you, and no one else.

What could be better than appreciation? Better than saying thank you and being grateful? Validation. Validation not only expresses your gratitude, but it also makes the person feel even better. Validation is thanking people for who they are. Telling people how amazing they are. Validation is better than any gift.

Value is what humans crave the most. When people feel valuable, they feel that they have a purpose, and reaching their purpose is what guides them.

Highest Form of Appreciation - Validation

Validation makes people smile, and there is truly no bigger satisfaction than a genuine smile that you have caused. You have made that person happier. You have affected their whole day by validating them. Validation is such a special concept because it is so simple, yet makes such a big difference in the world.

Validation is thanking people for who they are and not what they did. Being is the key word while validating. When you validate, you have to say, "Thank you" for being who you are. For example, if someone gives you a gift, validation would be saying, "Wow, thank you so much for being so thoughtful and buying me a gift! You are so kind!" Clearly, this would make the person feel good about themself.

What do you think? If someone said this to you instead just a thank you, wouldn't you feel extra special?

This is the highest stage of appreciation because it has the most impact, and it is also the hardest to do. It takes creativity to think of a word to describe the person in the moment. That is why people have a hard time validating.

But don't worry. That's not going to be you. I have a secret way to come up with a word in the moment.

Validation Made Easy

You don't have to do it in the moment! That's the secret! All you have to do is think of 3 words in advance that could work in any situation. You could use any of the following:

- Thoughtful
- Special
- Incredible
- Extraordinary
- Generous

All of these words would work in any situation, whether it is holding the door for you, giving a great presentation, or handing you a gift.

When validating someone, the word, "wow" is your best friend. Wow is such an incredible word, and if you are telling him or her "wow," they feel good because you have used such a powerful word to describe them.

The Impact of Validation

People feel confident when they get validated. Feeling confident is the road to success. Once you feel confident, you feel determined that you can do something. Validation gives people confidence like nothing else. It can make someone feel amazing and valuable. People will respect you more, and remember that you liked them doing something for you, so they will do it again.

If you are still finding validating someone difficult, then let me show you a great starting point. The easiest form of validation is self-validation. An easy way to start being able to validate is looking in the mirror once in a while and validating *yourself*. You can't give others validation unless you are validated yourself.

My Validation Ritual

Every morning what I like to do is grab a seat in front of the mirror, set a timer for three minutes, and just compliment myself. Whether it's saying, "Wow, thank you for being so caring towards your little brother," or "Yesterday you were so thoughtful when you gave your friend a gift," it helps me so much.

Validating myself makes me feel fresh, and I feel as if no obstacle can bother me. Validation helps me while complimenting others because I can use the same compliments that I validated myself with! Validating myself in the morning also reminds me of how amazing I am. This can really help some people, if they have no one who can validate them.

Getting validation from yourself is more important than getting validation from anyone else in the world. It doesn't matter if others compliment you. That always comes second. Always put validating yourself first. This not only boosts your confidence, but it also makes it easier to solve problems. If you are faced with a challenging situation, just remember the amazing things that you said about yourself, and remember how lucky you are to be you.

The Big NO

Never, ever, ever expect a validation from someone else. There are three main reasons why:

1. You could be expecting a big validation and not realizing the little compliments people give you, which are very valuable.

2. You could be let down because the validation you receive is the opposite of what you wanted, and could make you in a bad mood. Or even worse, you don't receive any type of validation and you are not happy in any way.

3. You are giving your personal strength to the person you are seeking validation from, and becoming weak for someone that doesn't deserve to have power over you.

Validation and Relationships

The other thing you can do to get validated is ask for it. If you share a good relationship with another person, it means that they have that much respect for you and you are able to ask a question and get a positive answer.

If you are still seeking validation from the person, it is not a good relationship. A good relationship wouldn't keep you waiting. Think about it. How much good would you get out of a relationship where the other person doesn't value you? Probably nothing. Instead of staying in those time-wasting relationships, where you have to beg for validation, make new relationships with people who value you and express their gratitude toward you being in their life.

"Life is too short to spend time with people who suck the happiness out of you."
Dr. Steve Maraboli

If you are constantly looking for approval from the people you are spending time with, they are draining the happiness out of you. You should always be happy, and if you cannot be because of the people around you, it's time to move out of your comfort zone and look for different friends.

This can be hard to do, especially if you have been friends for a long while. It's okay to let people go sometimes, because that's when you will really know if they care about you. If they notice you distancing yourself, and do something about it like invite you over, then you have to tell them the truth. If they realize that they have hurt you, they will make it up to you by validating you.

Again, never expect validation. Never try to force people to compliment you. It will not work. You have to keep it unexpected, because that is when it will impact you and make you happy.

Self-Validation

You don't need others' validation to feel valuable. All you need is your own encouragement. I want you to repeat these words over and over until you truly believe what you are saying:

I am an amazing person. I am so incredible! I don't need anyone else's approval. My opinion is the only one that counts. I am irreplaceable. I am grateful to be me and grateful to have my life the way it is right now.

Wow. You are powerful now. Do you feel that strength growing all over? You have a superpower now. Believe it or not. You have powers stronger than Superman. Courage, Uniqueness, and Confidence. All three! Wow.

Can you imagine feeling this powerful everyday? You would be a superhero to not only you, but also everyone you interact with. That is the strength of validation. Every morning, I want you to look in the mirror for only three minutes and either say the above words, or come up with your own:

____

____

____

Throwback Validation

Do you remember those "Great Job" stickers you got as a kid when you did a good job on a test or finished your homework? Do you remember when the teacher called you up in front of the whole class and gave you a small, shiny, gold star for being a good student and on top of the class? That was validation. Think of the proud, cheerful feelings you felt when accepting your "award." You probably will even remember the person or teacher who rewarded you with the sticker.

This just shows how significant that event was for you, because you got validated. You remember those few moments of being treated special. This is not unusual. It is very easy to remember those moments of validation.

Start Validating!

Let's talk about more recent incidents. When was a recent time you got validated? Appreciated for being who you are? Complimented for being the special you? Please take a moment and think about this.

Now, think about the different situations when you have validated someone. Have you validated someone recently?

If you are like most people, you have realized that validation is not common. Take a step out of the sea of sameness and START VALIDATING! You will immediately see the enormous benefits that come from validation.

Validation can cause miracles, and the sad thing is that many people don't do it. Why? Because they either are scared, or they don't know what it is! Being scared is not uncommon. When you first start, you feel like everyone is judging you. It is a part of human nature to think about others' criticism. To think about what others think about you. You have to be able to program yourself not to think about that, so that you can start validating. Don't worry about if people are staring or making nasty remarks. It's none of their business. They should be encouraging you for making a difference in someone's life. Just focus on that one person and compliment them.

As you start validating, you will start seeing its impact on you and those around you. Getting to do this on a regular basis may not be easy. Let us explore in further detail who, what, where, when, why, and how compliments can help.

Notes

Notes

Notes

Notes

Chapter 8

THE POWER OF A COMPLIMENT

"A compliment is verbal sunshine."
Robert Orben

Everyone has those days when we're feeling a little off, or tired, or down. Something bad has happened to us, or we are just sad or cranky. The only way to get out of that state of mind is to give a compliment to the first person you see. It sounds easier than it actually is, because on those bad days, it seems like of all the people, *you* have that rain cloud on your head following you around. You have to let someone know you like their outfit, or make them feel like they did something good that impacted you.

This will make their day brighter, and they will return the favour and make you happy as well. Who knows, they might've had the rain cloud following them too. Just saying a few positive words to someone made two rain clouds go away, made the sun shine, and made it happier for both of you. It can be hard to think of a compliment when you are having a bad day; because all you can think of is that dark cloud and everything negative in the world. All you have to do is look around at your environment. Look at the trees that provide oxygen. Look at the strangers who smile at you. Put your hand on your pulse. AND JUST BE GRATEFUL. Be grateful that you have oxygen to live. You have people around you to support you. You have a heart that beats in order for you to live. Everything is incredible. Now your dark, stormy, depressing cloud is no longer present. It is a colourful, positive, and beautiful rainbow.

Pay it Forward

Now that you have a rainbow, you have to give everyone else a rainbow. How do you do that? Compliments. Your compliment can't be something that will offend them in any way. It has to make the person feel good, or validated. In order to say a compliment that validates, you have to be able to construct one.

Good Compliment Defined

There are six characteristics of a good compliment:

1. **Any size-** Your compliment can be anything. It can be something huge like, *"Wow, you have a heart of gold,"* or something so small like, "Wow, I like your dress." Both of these compliments can change someone's entire day. Either one would change the way the person looked at themselves, and you.

2. **Make it unexpected-** The best compliments are random. You can't wait for the perfect moment to say something positive. It might even make the conversation flow smoothly and you will have a topic to talk about. With a stranger, you won't be strangers anymore. With friends, it will lead to a conversation that both of you will be interested in.

3. **Be specific-** General compliments aren't bad things, but being specific is always better. A detailed compliment will mean much more than just a general admiration. By focusing on something detailed, it shows your interest and curiosity in the other person.

4. **Genuine-** The most effective compliments are genuine. You have to make sure that you truly believe what you are saying. People can usually tell when you are being honest, and they appreciate it. Don't be brutally honest or exaggerate. When someone makes you pasta say, "This pasta is amazing. It has a really nice flavour." Don't say, "This is the best pasta I've ever had" because you are lying and exaggerating.

5. **Effort and Effect-** If you are complimenting the person, they have put some effort into whatever it is. They will like your compliment even more if you acknowledge that effort. It shows you realize the effort that they put into whatever you said about them. You also have to express how what you complimented them on affected *you*. For example, if someone gives a really informative presentation, you have to tell them that not only did you like it, but it taught you a lot. People like knowing that they are making a difference in the world and in people's lives.

6. **Unique-** Your compliment has to be unique. It can't be something obvious that they probably hear a lot. Don't tell a smart person you like their thinking. Don't tell a model you like their looks. Tell them something unexpected. Something they have never heard. Being

unique is a challenge, but it will set your compliment apart from others, and it'll have a bigger impact on the person. This can be difficult because you have to pay attention to the little details about people. It takes creative thinking. Again, this is why appreciation is an art.

The Boomerang Effect

Compliments are a genuine act of kindness. Although you are giving someone something, it doesn't mean you don't get anything in return. Never expect anything in return, because you will only get something if you leave the universe to do its purpose.

You can get a lot from giving. You get to meet new people and improve your relationships. According to the Merriam-Webster dictionary, a stranger is, "someone who you have not met before or do not know; someone is in a new and unfamiliar place." No one wants to be treated like a stranger. Everyone, no matter if they show it or not, wants to feel comfortable and not judged.

How do you bridge the gap between being strangers and friends? Validation through compliments. Most people are friendly, so you want to have conversations with strangers.

A compliment is a perfect way to start a conversation with a stranger. You never know what that person might become in the future. Everyone knows you can't foresee the future. They could be one of the best relations you've ever had. They could have exactly what you're looking for, whether it's a job opportunity, strong relationship, or just a positive conversation.

This bridge will help you in so many ways. It is a big step, but if you take it, you will get to the other side. And everyone knows the other side is better. The other side has positivity, friendships, and happiness. The most difficult part of the journey about building relationships is the initiative. If you have the courage to take a step on that bridge, you're already halfway there. Compliments can work wonders for you.

Even though there are so many amazing things about compliments, people are still scared to start a conversation with strangers. They are scared that they will be embarrassed or it will not turn out well. There is a small chance that it could go a different way than you wanted.

Word of Caution

Don't trust everyone you see. Don't tell them every secret you have. Just compliment them and see what they are like. Usually you can tell if a person is kind or strange by their response to a compliment. If you still can't make out what they are like, ask them a question. If you complimented them on something they are wearing, ask them where they got it. If they reply in a negative way, then don't continue to talk to them. But you can't expect for it to be bad. You have to be positive and hope that the person is nice.

Don't expect people to have time to talk to you if you see them in a rush. If they barely have time to fix their tie, I doubt they have time to converse with a stranger. If you try to have a long conversation, they will treat you poorly and you will be filled with regret. If people are in a rush, just smile at them and let them be.

Stranger Danger?

Change your perspective on things. Strangers are just friends that we don't know yet. The concept of "Stranger Danger" is such a vague concept. Strangers aren't all bad. You have to be able to look from someone else's perspective and be open-minded about talking to someone who could be in your future.

Children are learning the wrong definition of stranger through "Stranger Danger." They learn that strangers are bad people who you have to stay away from. Though it might be true in some cases, it should not be generalized. The media scares parents through fiction stories and out of fear, and then parents teach their children that anyone who they do not know is dangerous and will be harmful. This is sad.

All friends were past strangers. We weren't born with everyone in our lives. There must've been some type of interaction between you to have the relationship you have right now. That interaction is the key to everything. The perfect way to start that interaction is compliments. It's an automatic positive start.

The Other Side of the Coin

Let's look at the situation from the other side. Think of a compliment as a gift. If you are receiving a gift, you have to react to it positively. You have to be able to receive it well.

Believe it or not, accepting compliments is one of the hardest things about appreciation. People have a hard time accepting because they try to be modest. Being modest doesn't mean you have to deny all good things that happen to you. When some people get complimented, they downplay the compliment or straight up reject it. This can end the conversation immediately.

When you deny, deflect, or insult yourself, people think you are ungrateful or insecure. Gratitude is the only way you should react to a compliment. People are afraid of showing pride or vanity. Thankfulness does the opposite. It shows that you appreciate their awareness.

Here are three tips on how to accept compliments gratefully:

1. Say, *"Thank you."* It's so small, but it means so much. It shows your gratitude in a way like no other. Make sure

you say why you are grateful. For example, if someone says, *"I liked your presentation"* don't deny it and say, *"It wasn't that good, I did it in a rush."* Instead say, *"Thank you for your approval."*

2. Don't try to make your compliment better than theirs. Steer clear from the desire to let your competitive side come out and try to beat their compliment. Most people think that this is good, because you are returning the favour of spreading the love, but it makes the conversation more awkward and it makes it hard for the other person because they won't know how to respond.

3. Show interest in their opinion. When someone compliments you, immediately say thank you and than ask them a question based on what they said about you. For example, if someone complimented you on your presentation, ask, *"What was your favourite part?"*

Compliments are not that complicated, but people often get confused on how to give and receive compliments. Not you. You are the expert of compliments now.

Notes

Notes

Notes

Notes

Chapter 9

HABITS OF APPRECIATION

Wow. That was a lot of information. How are you going to use everything from eight whole chapters? Habits. Habits are so important in life because they are something that you do without thinking about it. Habits motivate you to be the best you can be. They help you use your time wisely. The following is an article by Jack Canfield:

Appreciation is one of the highest emotional states you can experience. When you cultivate gratitude, you're able to feel true joy and contentment, no matter what you have or *don't* have in your life. And since the Law of Attraction states that like attracts like, when you're grateful for what you already have, you will naturally attract more for which you can be grateful.

However, many people find that it requires great diligence to cultivate a persistent attitude of appreciation. That's because we've been culturally conditioned to focus on what we don't have, rather than appreciating what we've already received or achieved.

To help you combat this conditioning, here are 6 simple tips on how to make gratitude a natural part of your daily routine, and so you can attract more joy and abundance into your life all year long:

1. **Take 7 minutes each morning to write down everything you appreciate in life**

   Starting your day this way primes you to be receptive and grateful for everything your day will bring. It also helps you cultivate an air of positivity that makes you naturally more attractive to other positive people – and inspires them to want to help you achieve your goals.

2. **Make a conscious effort to appreciate at least 3 people every day**

   By letting people know how much you appreciate them, you increase their own sense of appreciation and self-worth, and encourage them to pay this positive energy forward to other people.

While most people enjoy receiving verbal appreciation, written notes are also nice because they can be saved and re-read. (For ideas on expressing appreciation, grab your copy of *The Success Principles* and review Principle 53: Practice Uncommon Appreciation.)

3. **Play the Appreciation Game**

Set a specific time each day to consciously appreciate everything you encounter. An ideal time to do this is on your way to or from work. Appreciate the people you pass, the road you walk on, the cars that let you merge into a different lane, the street signs that make it easy for you to know where you're going, the rain that's nourishing the plants and trees, and so on.

Look for the good in all situations – even those you would normally view as negative. As the saying goes, "Every cloud has a silver lining." For example, when my wife was in a car accident a few years ago, she could have chosen to berate herself or question her judgment. Instead, she focused on her gratitude for suffering only minor injuries and for the help she received from other drivers.

4. **Carry a physical token of gratitude in your pocket, such as a heart-shaped stone, crystal, or some other small item**

   A physical reminder can bring you back to your practice of gratitude when your mind has drifted elsewhere. As you reach into your pocket throughout the day and feel the token, use it as a reminder to stop, breathe and take a moment to fully experience the emotion of gratitude. The more conscious effort you put into seeking it out, the easier it will be to find it – and the more powerful your experience will be.

5. **Remember to appreciate the smallest blessings**

   The best way to activate your gratitude is by acknowledging the gifts most people take for granted. If you have food in your refrigerator, clothes in your closet and a roof over your head, you are better off than 75 % of the world's population.

   If you eat three meals a day, you are far better off than the 1 billion people on the planet who eat once a day at most.

Do you have a phone? How about a car that allows you to travel to work or to explore the country? Is your family healthy? Do you have a computer and Internet access to stay in touch with the world, get access to education, and perform work for which you are paid? Do you have clean water to drink?

Celebrate these simple blessings. These daily conveniences are gifts that most people in the world do not enjoy.

6. **Appreciate yourself**

Finally, don't forget to appreciate your OWN positive qualities and accomplishments. In addition to celebrating your big successes, acknowledge your small daily successes too. We all need acknowledgement, but the most important acknowledgement is that which we give ourselves.

One of the most powerful ways to acknowledge and appreciate yourself is by doing the Mirror Exercise. This powerful exercise requires you to appreciate yourself for the day's accomplishments while talking to yourself in a mirror. For detailed instructions and guidance for the Mirror Exercise, see page 199-201 of *The Success Principles.*

It may not feel natural at first to focus on appreciating what you already have, but by faithfully practicing the Daily Appreciation Habits outlined in this article, you'll begin to change your conditioning.

To kick-start your daily gratitude practice, take a few moments to share at least three things for which you're grateful for in the comments. Even the smallest act of gratitude will have a positive impact on your life.

http://jackcanfield.com/6-daily-gratitude-habits-that-will-attract-more-abundance-and-joy-into-your-life/

Notes

Notes

Notes

Notes

Chapter 10

TAKE ACTION

"Gratitude is the rent you pay to live on Earth."
Les Brown

Now that you know the importance of appreciation and how it impacts you and people around you, let's go the last and final step. Here are 50 things that you can be grateful for:

1. Air- we have oxygen that lets us breathe freely

2. Nature- we have beautiful trees and plants that make our world colourful and fresh.

3. The sun- the bright gleam of light that shines on you no matter what happens it is something that should not be taken for granted

4. The moon and stars- for glowing in the night sky and looking breathtaking

5. The rain- dancing in the rain, splashing in puddles, letting little drops roll down windows; it's magical

6. Snow- making your winters so much better by snowball fights or catching snowflakes on your tongue

7. Animals- we have so much diversity in the world, and the beauty in every species is so unique

8. Water- to keep you fresh, and to have access to it whenever you get thirsty

9. Food- so much food, so little time

10. Shelter- to keep you safe and warm when you need it the most

11. Clothing- for keeping you covered and in proper temperature

12. Transportation- to get from point A to B so much faster than walking

13. Internet- for any information that you need, any time

14. Technology- for being so advanced and helping you in times that you need something

15. Phones- for being reliable and having so many applications for everything

16. Movies- for entertaining you

17. Books- for teaching you knowledge

18. Music- for having so much variety and elevating your mood

19. Your bed- for having somewhere to sleep peacefully

20. Your home- for being able to do what you want without being judged

21. Your family- for loving you no matter what

22. Y0ur parents- for giving birth to you and raising you to be the person you are today

23. Your siblings- for giving such special experiences while growing up with them.

24. Your friends- for supporting you and being by your side

25. Your school- for teaching you and giving you knowledge to use throughout life

26. Teachers- for dedicating their time and effort to you

27. Your job- for showing you how you are making a difference

28. Sense of touch- for being able to feel the breeze of the winds, hugs from loved ones, and high fives from achievements

29. Sense of smell- for letting you smell flowers, candles and food

30. Sense of sight- for being able to see life and the amazing beauty of everything around you

31. Sense of taste- for letting you eat and having to decide the differences between spicy, sweet, or salty

32. Sense of hearing- being able to hear the birds chirping or the people around you or the amazing music

33. Your reading ability- you are able to read these sentences so easily and it gives you so much knowledge

34. Your speech- to have a unique voice to say what you believe in and share your ideas

35. Your hands- for letting you flip the pages in this book, type words on a computer, snap, clap, and get through the day

36. Your legs- for letting you move with ease

37. Your lungs- for holding the oxygen so that you can breathe

38. Your heart- for pumping blood to all the parts of your body to stay healthy

39. Your mind- to have a brain to process the experiences, make decisions, control emotions, and much more

40. Your health- for letting you do what you do

41. Kind strangers- for lighting up any day

42. Your mistakes- for helping you become a better person

43. Tears- for letting you appreciate how good it feels to be happy

44. Disappointment- to let you know the things that matter the most

45. Pain- for becoming a stronger person

46. Happiness- for life's amazing moments

47. Laughter- for the most satisfying feeling that makes you feel warm and fuzzy and experience joy in life

48. Love- for letting you feel what it means to be alive

49. Life- for everything and everyone

50. You- you are unique and you should be thankful you are yourself and nobody else

Every single person in the world is blessed. We are blessed to have so much. Blessed to be alive in this generation. Blessed to live on planet Earth. Wow.

Gratitude is the only thing that you have to give in order to live happily. If you are able to be grateful for everything, you will be happy with your life. On the saddest days, you need to look at life from a different perspective and appreciate your own perspective.

It All Fits

"The seed of goodness is found in the soil of appreciation."
Dalai Lama

If you want to be good, and have a good attitude, you have to be appreciative. If you can't appreciate, then the seed of goodness and happiness will not grow. And that seed is the plant of life.

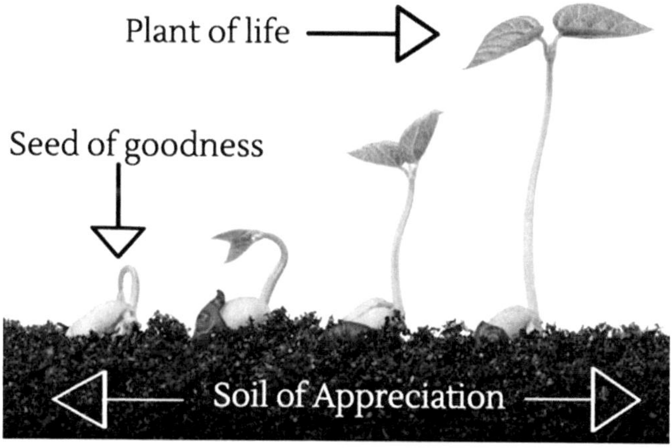

The Appreciation Action Plan

In order to appreciate everything and everyone, I have started a system called 365 grateful. At the back of this book, there is a chart for a few pages for your own 365 grateful. Every day, I write a one-sentence thank you note to what I am thankful for. There are unlimited things in the world, and you could be grateful for absolutely anything. Another thing that will help you conquer a bad day is the appreciation checklist. The appreciation checklist is not a to do list. It's not like any other checklist. It is a unique checklist that you will find nowhere else. This checklist has 20 actions that you can do to show your gratitude in the world. All you have to do is pick five items every day, and do them. Try to keep each day different, because it will add more variety to your life. Please note that these are just a few examples. However, you can decide to come up with your own list.

"What if you woke up with only the things
you thanked god for yesterday?"
Michael Hyatt

This is one of my favourite quotes in the entire world. It makes me think and reminds me what a big necessity it is to appreciate everything and everyone. Think about this quote. Think about the day before you started reading this book. How many things had you thanked? How many people did you genuinely thank?

Now, I would encourage you to fill out this gratitude journal every day, and see how it affects your life.

Morning gratitude Before you begin your day, list 10 things you're grateful for 1. 2. 3. 4. 5. 6. 7. 8. 9. 10.	**What I'm learning from my challenges** List three obstacles and what you're learning from them 1. What I'm learning: 2. What I'm learning: 3. What I'm learning:

People I'm grateful for List 5 people who made your life a little happier today. (These could be friends, family, or strangers) 1. 2. 3. 4. 5.	**The best part of my day** Choose one moment from your day that made you happy and focus on it for 5 minutes before bed

The world can be dark at times. We need more light. You can be the light that shines in the darkness and spreads like fire. If someone is having a bad day, you validate him or her. You can light up their world so they will spread the light to other people. Appreciation is the key to having a brighter world.

"In a world filled with hate, we must still dare to hope
In a world filled with anger, we must still dare to comfort.
In a world filled with despair, we must still dare to dream
And in a world filled with distrust,
we must still dare to believe."
Michael Jackson

Notes

Notes

Notes

Notes